Healing Angel
and Other Poems

Irene M Stead

ATHENA PRESS
LONDON

ISBN 10-digit: 1 84748 035 7
ISBN 13-digit: 978 1 84748 035 4

First Published 2007 by
ATHENA PRESS
Queen's House, 2 Holly Road
Twickenham TW1 4EG
United Kingdom

Printed for Athena Press

This book is dedicated to Mum, Dad, John, Lee-Anne and all my dear friends and helpers in the higher realms who have been my inspiration. Also to my daughters, Joanne and Kellie-Anne, and my darling granddaughter, Olivia Rose Treas.

Contents

Healing Angel

Go walk among the angels,
Until you earn your wings.
Go walk among the angels,
And learn of many things.

Go walk among the angels,
And tell how you were loved.
Go walk among the angels,
With our Father up above.

Go walk among the angels,
And take a well-earned rest.
Go walk among the angels,
For you are truly blessed.

Go walk among the angels,
Your time with us is done.
Go walk among the angels,
Your rewards are yet to come.

Bright Star

You were such a bright, bright star,
You shone out wherever you were.
Oh so good and the peaceful kind
In this day so hard to find.

When we look at the sky by night
You are like a bright new light,
Shining out for all to see,
Knowing what you mean to me.

So go and shine, my bright
New star,
You'll be with us always,
Wherever you are.

Just a Woman

Take a look, stand back, tell me what you see.
I am a human being,
Just a woman, this is me.
I'm flesh and blood, with feelings;
I've no magic to perform,
I don't have all the answers,
I never said I did.
Stand back and take a look,
This is what you see:
I am just a woman,
A mother, a grandmother,
I'm really only human.
I get tired, I get stressed,
There are even times I get depressed.
So take a closer, longer look,
I'm a woman,
I am me.

Love

Happy is the child
Who feels loved, right from the start.
Happy is the child
That feels love within his heart.
Happy is the child
When love shines there in his eyes.
Happy is the child
Who has parents who are wise.
Happy is the child
Who feels loved every day.
Happy is the child
Who feels protected, in this way.
Happy is the child
A precious gift, sent from above.
Happy is the child
That has been truly blessed with love.

Fresh Breath

The winds of change are blowing,
All across the Earth.
A new time is coming, a new era and rebirth.
It's coming soon, and swiftly.

Like a mighty furious gale,
The winds of change will show man
That this folly can no longer prevail.
The changes they are coming fast.

And man will have to pay
For the way he's been disrespectful
To Mother Nature, to name one.
The might of man's powerful hand,

Use to rise up and then destroy.
The way the earth has been misused,
Dear children, innocent, so abused,
Man will have to answer.

Tall majestic trees of green,
Thick rich forests, now unseen.
Lush vegetation, no more around,
Many rainforests burned to the ground.

The winds of change are coming,
Yes they are on their way.
Mother Nature cries out in pain,
And she will have her day.

Time will Heal

When you lose a loved one
And try to understand,
You need someone there beside you,
To care and hold your hand.

Someone who will listen,
And show you lots of love,
And share with you the feelings,
That make you angry and so sad.

And through all this confusion,
You wonder if you're mad.
Then someone to support you,
Can hold you up so high.

Being there, just for you,
To help you when you cry.
Letting out that inner pain
Takes a long, long time.

Knowing that things
Will never be the same,
But time, and love,
Fades away the pain.

My Other Senses

The colours of the rainbow
Are just as bright to me.
They're warm and soft and vivid,
Although I cannot see.

I have four other senses
That are sharpened like a knife.
They are waiting here to serve me,
To help me through my life.

My taste buds up, raring to go,
Until I taste I do not know.
Good food there upon my plate,
Smelling good, I just can't wait!

Feels like silk, what can compare,
As I sit and brush my hair?
Just running it through my fingers,
How that softness lingers.

Smell a friend within a room,
By her sweet fragrant perfume.
Rich red roses please my nose,
In a vase they proudly pose.

Sweet violins the music play,
Lay back, relax, on a summer's day.
Hear the trickling of the rain,
Soft vibrations on the window pane.

Orange, pinks, and vivid blues
Dazzle my mind, so many to choose.
When someone says a colour to me,
Magnificent spectrum, in my mind.

My eyes may be closed to what you see,
But I have so much here with me.
I see this spectrum here inside,
Fantasy colours I can't describe.

I try not to question
What happened to me.
I just live my life and try to be
As the Lord intended, and do all I can
To live in love and peace with my fellow man.

To the Best – From the Best

Oh my dearest darling,
I've been missing you so much.
I miss you here by my side,
And your warm and loving touch.

As the days come and go
And I stop to think of you,
All the love comes flooding back,
A love so rich and true.

All the years we had together,
Sharing both our lives,
The ups, the downs, they came and went,
You, my dear, were heaven-sent.

Our golden years, so soon to pass,
The love we shared was meant to last.
Joined in trust and love together,
Our love will live on for ever.

Bright green leaves upon a tree,
Sunshine and roses when you think of me.
God bless you in all you do;
My caring husband, I love you.

These things make you Happy

A smile upon a child's face,
Hills of green, a quiet place;
These things make you happy.

The colours on a painting bright,
To try and try then get it right;
These things make you happy.

Pretty flowers in a row,
Sitting back to watch them grow;
These things make you happy.

Sweet coolness of the summer rain
Then the sun comes out again;
These things make you happy.

Pastel colours, rich deep blue,
Important words like 'I love you';
These things make you happy.

Birds about to fly on by,
Soft white clouds up in the sky;
These things make you happy.

Lovely rainbows way up high
Beauty that does please the eye;
These things make you happy.

Kind eyes and a wagging tail,
A friendship that will never fail;
These things make you happy.

All the seasons come and go,
Warm bright sunshine, then falls snow;
These things make you happy.

A Silent World

This child's ears are not perfect.
My heart is filled with pain.
He may never hear the birds sing
Or the trickle of the rain.

He may never hear the wind
As it rustles through the trees,
He may never hear the scrunching
As he walks among the leaves,
Nor the voices of loved ones
Telling how they are proud and pleased.

He may never hear a haunting tune
Played sweetly on a harp;
The bleating of a newborn lamb,
Its life about to start.

Please God, may his hearing be aided
As he goes upon his way,
So he can hear the sounds on Earth
That we take for granted every day.

May he hear, one day, his mother's voice
When she tells him how she loves him.
O dear Lord, may he hear the wonders of our world –
The mighty thunder crash and roar,
A chirping bird, a slamming door.

Please bless his ears with all these sounds
That every day do us surround.
Our Earth is such a wonderful place,
Please put a smile upon his face.

Amen.

Road to Victory

As you go on from day-to-day
You'll find the courage,
You'll find a way.
There's someone to guide you
With each step you take,
He'll look over
And keep you
With each move you make.

May your courage and strength
Grow stronger each day,
Till the fight you have fought
Has been fought –
And you've won.

Some days are long
And some are short,
So make the best of each new one.

Nurse

Nurse, we call you angel,
With your tender loving care.
We, the family members,
Are so grateful you are there.

To tend and help our loved ones
With your love and tender touch;
It takes a special person,
To care so very much.

It eases our great burden,
And gives us a small break,
Knowing there is so much care,
And an angel when they wake.

God bless and keep you always,
May you find the strength each day
To carry on the caring
In your very special way.

Conscience

The purest, freshest innocence,
Like a spirit just been born.
Like a soft spring lamb,
For the first time to be shorn.

The purest, freshest glow of light,
The dazzling glint of snow so bright.
The inner self that has that tingle,
Like the freedom when a person's single.

The purest glow of shimmering light,
That shines within, so strong and bright.
The inner self that knows what's right.
When we do wrong, it is our plight.

Let the Music Flow

Sweetly play that music
On the keys of black and white,
Softly, ever flowing,
Into the silence of the night.

Ever gently flowing,
As the notes join into one.
Sweetly play the music
As the words are sweetly sung.

Let the music flow
From the talent in your hands,
Like the soft, warm, golden,
Flowing grains of sand.

You will be surrounded by love
Everywhere you go.
So play the sweet, sweet music,
And know we love it so.

You help to lift our hearts
As we sing thanks to him.
The air is filled with music,
Like an ever-flowing stream.

As the music plays,
And we walk through the door,
You fill our hearts with so much love,
Could we ever ask for more?

Wake Up to the Light

Don't wander all alone
And lost within the dark.
Remember how the bright star shone
And there was light all around.

Open up your heart inside
And feel the glowing warmth.
Once the truth is all around,
It's very hard to hide.

Share now in this mighty glow,
Join with us that all might know
The power of the mighty light.
Open up your heart, that it may shine bright.

Feel this bright glow inside,
This mighty power, feel the pride.
A heart that's bursting full of joy;
Turn the light on, good and bright,
Walk the right path, know what's right.

Life Goes On

Oh! What joy wells up in me,
When I know you're safe,
And now pain free.
My heart it beats a happy tune,

Knowing I'll hear from you soon.
Sitting still in my sanctuary,
Being told how you loved me;
Messages from the other side.

Oh! So near and yet so far.
Just for you to touch my hand;
But I know you're there
And you understand.

How my heart still longs for you,
I remember silly things we used to do.
How my heart fills full of love,
When I think of you with the ones we love.

How I'm lifted so up high,
These are tears of joy I shed.
You are not so far away,
And together once more we'll be one day.

He Only Came to Save Us

What did they do
When they crowned you with thorns,
Sharp and so piercing;
Treated you with scorn?

How could they mock and be so cruel,
When here stood a man, so perfect and tall?
Inside, his heart was bursting with love,
Blessed and given by his Father above.

How could they treat him so unkind and unjust,
When here stood a man with nothing but trust?
Oh! How those thorns pierced deep in his head,
The deeper they went, the more he bled.

He spilled his blood,
And his life slipped away.
Have we learned?
How would we greet him today?

Message with Love

It's nice to write a letter,
And send your love upon its way.

To cheer and make someone happy,
And brighten up their day.

To say how much you care,
And you're glad that they are there.

A letter's so worthwhile,
When it makes the reader smile.

And they know they've just
Received a little love!

Wing and a Prayer

O serene bright angel,
Spread your silver wings.
Carry all the messages,
Our prayers and special things.

Look over us while we're asleep,
Take care of us, with love so deep.
Guard us each and every day.
Give us the strength, that we won't stray.

Thank you, angel, shining bright,
May we be on the path that's right.
Like a star shining bright above,
Spread your wings and spread your love.

Many people everywhere
Thank you for your help and care.
Graceful angels be abound,
Thank you for being around.

As we sleep and you guard our bed,
Cast your light around our head.
Soft bright light spreads warmth around,
Gently we sleep; hearing not a sound.

Warmth Within

I see the face of a lonely man
With so much love to share.
Gentle sweetness, good and kind,
But there's no one there to care.

No one to share his laughter,
And sometimes share a tear.
No one he can call upon,
To know that they are near.

He may feel lonely, but he has been blessed,
With heart that's loving and free.
This man would make a valued friend,
If eyes were only open to see.

So much has been wasted,
I wish he'd come to me.
Then I could learn so much –
Put out my hand and value his touch.

That's all we ever want: to care.
Eyes making contact, then a warm smile,
To make a friend, and know it's worthwhile.
Loneliness is a desolate thing.

Like a permanent cold winter,
With no sign of spring.
Look into a lonely man's sad eyes,
Who knows, you might get a nice surprise.

And make a friend who's there for you,
With love and support in all you do.
But, best of all, it's the beginning, not end,
Of having, and making, a really good friend.

High Hopes

If only man could live in peace,
And wars and silly conflicts cease.
Then we could live our lives so calm,
Our brothers then would meet no harm.

War, thrust upon a mundane life,
Drags us into hate and strife.
If only we could live in peace,
And all out discontents release.

Ever happy, feeling no woe –
What a dream, if only this!
No more fist, but gentle kiss.
If only man could live in peace.

To speak gently, nice kind words,
Like the sweet chatter of the birds.
Maybe the world one day will be
At peace, and live in harmony.

Sharing

Spare a copper, learn to share,
Look deep within, compassion's there.
If you have so much, that you throw away,
Share with me on a hungry day.

A dustbin lid's like a vast fridge door,
Rich pickings to be had, but I'd like more:
A nice fresh loaf and a bowl of soup.
Once I was proud, but now I stoop.

I am no better or worse than you,
Life's just another challenge for me to get through.
One day I pray that my life will get fair,
Then I can look back and say, 'I've been there.'

I'd never forget that one day I was so low,
That I walked the streets with nowhere to go.
Then I would share all my knowledge,
'I've been there, I know.'

Heroes of the West

The Red Indians were a very proud race,
They put the warpaint on their face.
How they made the white man quake;
With their haunting cries, the earth did shake.

Stagecoach and the iron horse came
To disturb the balance of the plain.
The buffalo was fast to go,
He gave food and warmth against the snow.

Sickness and starvation took its toll,
The Indians saw very few friends.
No one tried to make amends
For the wrong that they had done
And the battle that they won.

They sat and smoked the pipes of peace,
The truce was short-lived, the peace did cease.
Rest, you mighty warriors, be found
'In the happy hunting ground.'

Don't Just Take

Some have plenty, others not enough,
Out on the streets it can really get tough.
The cold it bites into your bones,
The pain is dull and deep.

What I'd give for some cosy warmth
And a bed for me to sleep.
Just one room would be to me
Like a mansion, rich and fine.

And when I'm home and close the door,
The room and contents mine,
I'd make my tea, and have some toast,
To my friends be the perfect host.

A room for me, no more cold,
Sheltered from the sword-sharp wind.
So cosy in my warm snug room,
Ready to curl up and dream.

Innocents

All God's tiny children
Go on their knees to pray.
Sweet, innocent children,
Showing us the way.

Pure in their freshness,
They wake us up each day.
Sweet innocent children,
Showing us the way.

Gentle, smiling children,
Eyes so full of love.
God's little beings,
Sent from heaven above.

Dear, sweet, loving children,
Showing us the way.
May our eyes be opened,
May we see clear every day.

Paradise

There's a place in the sun
That I would love to run to.
A place that is fresh and warm,
Where you can lose your cares.

The sand is warm and golden,
Like the shimmer of the sun,
And the sea, with its mighty strength,
Comes lashing around your feet.

You lose that mighty feeling
And you feel quite petite.
The trees, they sway in harmony,
As the wind blows through their leaves.

So gentle, just like they're dancing
To a tune blown by the breeze.
Mother-of-pearl shells get washed up
And the colours catch the light.

Truly beautiful colours; truly sheer delight.
Such a place, here on Earth,
A paradise that's been kissed by the sun.
This is my ideal place, the place to which I'd run.

See you on a Summer's Day

I'll see you in the summertime,
When the roses bloom again.
You'll be walking in the sunshine,
Cooled by the sweet light rain.

You'll be standing among the flowers,
As the colours all kiss and caress you.
And I'll see you in all your beauty,
Remembering how much I love you.

You'll stand there right beside me,
And my breath you'll take away.
I will be oh so restless
Until that lovely summer's day.

Guiding Light

There's a candle in a window,
And it's shining out to me,
Giving light to all who pass by,
And peace to all that see.

There is a true sense of peace,
As the candle catches my eye,
Shining out so strong and bright,
Into the darkness of the night.

Giving out its gentle warmth,
Like a mother gives out her love,
Truly a most calming sight,
Sheer peace and pure delight.

Suffer the Little Children

Little children, feeling sad,
World of ours treats them bad.
Greedy people fail to share,
Although there is plenty there.

Why don't we learn to give
And in peace and love to live?
Oh what a happy earth plane,
If no more sad children, ever again.

Oh to close your eyes and dream,
What a truly ideal scene.
Eyes open wide, it doesn't last long.
What's the answer? What went wrong?

Storyteller

As I put my pen to paper
And write down all the words,
Imagination flows through my pen;
Find it hard to start, but then

Soon before me a story emerges,
Colourful adventure, happiness and tears.
Oh such smiles upon their faces,
Suitable for all the years.

Giving pleasure to the reader,
Sweet escape from life's many stresses.
Take them into bright adventure,
Lovely damsels, golden tresses.

From the first line to the last,
Big impression, enjoyed by all.
Storyteller's imagination
Fills a book and much pleasure brings.

Birthright

This is my home, the place of my birth,
My special corner here on the Earth.
I was sent to this special place.
This is my culture, this is my race.

I never chose to be black or white.
It's not my fault men want to fight.
I'd like to live in peace always,
Living my life with calm happy days.

Wasted time spent on futile wars,
When there is such knowledge
Behind so many doors.
There's so much to learn,

But we turn our back.
Hopefully, soon, we'll get back on track.
This is my home, my place on Earth,
It was entrusted to me.

Since the day of my birth.
It needs more respect,
Not to mention tender care,
For this beautiful planet

Has been passed down to share.
This is my home, I'm glad to be here,
And for all the beauty that I know.
To my planet, all I owe.

If we don't soon open up our eyes
And look at what we have,
With a blink it will all be gone.
What a sad and sorry refrain.

We are the caretakers of the Earth,
Shared with us since the day of birth
By sweet Mother Nature
And dear Mother Earth.

Peaceful Sanctuary

May your home be filled with love
And peace dwell there within.
May all who enter through the door
Feel the sanctuary therein.

Let the rooms be filled with love,
So strong from wall-to-wall,
Giving out a calmness
To be shared by one and all.

So let your home be welcoming,
With compassion and much love.
Feel reborn, afresh and new,
For our Father has blessed you.

He sets each day so many tests,
You were chosen, you were blessed.
So share your gift with one and all,
He's always there when you think you fall.

May God bless you every day,
As you go along your way,
And give you strength and inner peace;
Know that his love will never cease.

Bright Light

You are the light of my life
And you shine out for me.
You're all the goodness that I see,
Like beautiful flowers on a bright summer's day.

I never want you to go away.
Let's walk together on the path of life,
Going onward together
Against the pain and the strife.

Sharing all together, how it's meant to be.
I'll always be here for you,
And you'll always be here for me.
You are the light that shines so bright,
You are my morning, day and night.

You are the stars and the moon above,
Oceans so deep, like the depth of my love.
My love reaches up oh so high,
High up as the beautiful sky.

Masterpiece

I would write a picture,
Of blues and yellows and greens.
Bright and vivid words
To describe every scene.

Every word would be so clear,
And they would all fall into line.
This lovely picture made up of words
A feast for the eyes so divine.

Sit back and take a look
At this picture, oh so perfect.
The beauty and the colourful words,
Just like a puzzle with pieces blending.

If I could write a masterpiece,
What pleasure to the eye;
A picture written for all to share,
To lose yourself and just be there.

Delightful Features

If I could write a picture,
A picture of your face,
I'd write about your beauty
And your sweet gentle grace.

I'd write your eyes, oh so blue,
Just like the softness of the sky.
Your cheeks so red and rosy,
Like a sunset passing by.

I'd write your skin, so rich and fair,
The gold within your flowing hair.
And the beauty in this picture
Would be a stunning work of art.

Right Track

We walk along the rugged path,
It's hard to keep on track.
But we try to keep going,
So rarely looking back.

The road is hard and rough –
In places it gets real tough –
But on we trudge, knowing at the end
We will reach our goal.

As we tread the last steps
We feel proud, but weary.
We feel so happy,
With no regrets.

Indian Maiden

She stands there with her eyes so bright,
Her hair is soft like silk.
She really is so beautiful,
With skin as smooth as milk.

Truly blessed with beauty,
Like a precious work of art,
She has the stature of a queen;
Beauty like this is so rarely seen.

If only I could feast my eyes
On beauty rare as this –
Like the sun in the early morn,
When the Earth has just been kissed.

As the light through the trees shines
Just like a fresh golden sheen,
Only once in a lifetime
Is beauty like this seen.

Titanic, the Legend

How majestic she sailed away,
Never to return.
Just like a floating palace,
Now split from bow to stern.

All the people partied
As their new lives
Before them laid.
Just like the mighty atom bomb,

Disbelief left them dismayed.
All the cold and sorrow
Rich and poor alike did feel.
Quick to go was their laughter,

Their eagerness and their zeal.
She's laid upon the ocean floor
For oh so many years;
People heard in disbelief

And cried their bitter tears.
It wasn't supposed to sink like this,
And never to return.
Such anticipation with that parting kiss.

Now she's in the history books,
She lies between the pages.
A tragedy of human loss
Remembered through the ages.

Opened Eyes

Many times I've felt so sad,
Not realising all I had.
All the love, so sweet,
Surrounds me.

Happy, feeling loved and free,
Every day was just for me.
When it's gone and you look back,
Brightness turns to cold, sad black.

Then you know just what you had,
And deep inside you feel so sad.
As time passes and the pain does heal,
You remember the long forgotten.

Wishing you could relive again
All those things that flood on back.
Trying hard to keep on track
Thoughts of a lovely day.

Walking through a field of hay,
Forgetting all the sadness and pain,
Thoughts go back to summer rain.
Under-valued days go past,
Life goes by, it travels fast.

Closed

We walked beside the waters
As he did those years gone by.
He trod the path of beauty
As the wonder filled his eyes.

He came to tell of many things
To help us on our way,
He had a way about him
That cheered each break of day.

He passed on his Father's word,
So sacred and so wise.
But our eyes weren't fully opened,
And the truth was buried by lies.

He came upon the Earth for us
To teach us many wise things.
We saw him gently heal the sick,
With loving hands and kind words.

He only came to save us,
But we sent him back again.
He suffered for all our sins,
We gave him so much pain.

He was sweet and gentle,
But we nailed him to the cross.
His head did bleed from thorns so sharp,
His faith it never wavered.

For he knew his Father's love,
How in truth he was favoured.
The tears did flow when he rose again.
To his Father up above.

Then he came back once again,
To the friends who showed such love.
All their faith was strengthened now,
And the truth it would not bend.
They knew how much he loved them,
And this was not the end.

Linking Words

Linking words together,
Books go on for ever.
Knowledge lies within,
Every page is eagerly read.

Cosy, tucked up snug in bed,
Lose oneself among the words.
Sweet adventure fills my head,
Every time I turn a page.

Some are calm and some have rage,
Colourful stories grip my mind.
Takes me off and then I dream,
Such adventures fill each scene.

Learning and Growing

Sweet angelic little faces,
Playing hopscotch, winning races.
The days they start to go to school,
Have to learn and obey the rules.
Make new friends from this day on,
Tears and laughter, happy throng.
Learning things, day after day,
Helping them upon their way.

Lovely Memories

Lovely memories tinged with sadness,
Precious memories of our loved ones.
It seemed they'd be here for ever,
But oh, too soon, time goes by
And they are gone; our tears we cry.

We pick out the special days,
Love and laughter, such kind ways.
Warmth and smiles, our memories come,
Remembering all the days of fun.

Love overflows deep in our heart,
We regret the day we had to part.
All the memories we lock away,
Magic thoughts of our special days.

All those days we shared together,
Good and bad times we'd just weather.
Smiles and tears, so many years.

Love spent together, love you for ever.
On a day when I am blue,
I have my precious memories of you,
And I turn them over in my mind.

Like a book that's so valued,
And it's all yours and mine.
The memories are all recalled,
Sweet, gentle, precious memories, so divine.

Glow Within

You are the love that shines
From deep within my eyes.
You are the sweet anticipation
When there's a nice surprise.

You are every and all to me,
You are the all round beauty that I see.
You are the gentle essence of life,
You are everything for which I strive.

You are all that is to me,
And all that ever was to be.
You are a fresh breath every day,
My helping hand – you show the way.

You are the reason I survive,
Now I breathe, I feel alive.
You are my glow from deep inside,
You make my heart swell up with pride.

Harmony

Sweet meditation across every nation,
Sweetly calming the world.
Such gentle vibrations,
Reaching out to all the nations,
Joy to every boy and girl.

Peaceful and giving,
What a great way of living.
Smiles upon the faces,
Reaching out to all the races.
Peace all over the world.

Soft harmonising vibrations,
Peace to each and every nation.
Lifting hearts and spirits abound,
Sending out peace and love around.

Celestial Being

There's an extra star in the sky tonight,
It's shimmering out, so true and bright,
Showing us that life goes on,
Like the words of an old familiar song.

All around, for many miles to see,
Your love shines out to me.
Clear and bright, not far from my side,
I look to you with love and pride.

There's an extra star in the sky tonight,
It's pure and white, such a beautiful sight.
Guiding all those who want to see
The love we shared and what's meant to be.

Just like the colours in a crystal,
That shine so clear and bright.
I know that you watch over me,
And in time everything will be all right.

The joy we shared throughout the years,
Sharing laughter and sharing tears.
You were so loving, fresh and dear,
Here in my heart I hold you near.

Don't Bully, Be Kind

We must speak up, now, today,
We must speak up and show the way.
We must speak up and stop this hell,
We must speak up, be brave and tell.
We must find someone we can trust,
We must be brave, we simply must.
We must put these bullies in their place,
We must tell and make them lose face.
We must speak up, for our peace of mind,
We must speak up so they respect and they're kind.
We must speak up, now today,
We must speak up and show the way.

Look Around

Please slow down, I want to see
All the wonders that surround me.
We rush and tear about each day,
Get angry if someone's in our way.

Please slow down, then you will know
It's just the same if you go slow.
Take it easy, don't rush around,
Look about, see what will confound.

We miss so much as we dash around,
Don't have our feet on the ground.
Slow down and open your eyes,
Look around, have a nice surprise.

All this beauty given to you and me,
It's all out there for you to see.
Rush around it will come and go,
With eyes so closed you won't ever know.

You Are

You are the reason I survive,
You are the reason I'm alive.
You give me beauty every day,
You guide me and show the way.
You are the bird upon the wing,
You are the love in the song they sing.
You are the peace here on Earth,
You are the miracle of birth.
You are the life there in the trees,
You are the strength within the breeze.
You are the perfume in a flower,
You are the quietness in an hour.
You are the love within my heart,
You were my purpose from the start.
You are the green within the grass,
You help – I only have to ask.
You are a mountain high,
You are joy in the tears I cry.
You are all that is to me,
You are the reason, you help me see.
You are with me each and every day,
You are my all, you guide my way.
You are the reason.

If Only

If only we could be kind
And check our lashing tongues;
Think before we speak,
Never hurting precious feelings
To leave a battered heart.

If only we could learn to think
Before the words come out,
Before spilling out our anger
That makes us rant and shout.

If only we could think
Before the words come out,
Be kind and speak in peace,
No need to rant and rage and shout.

Legacy of Love

All the love I have in me,
Handed down through my family tree,
Built stronger through each generation,
Fills my heart with much adoration.

Ancestors of mine gone by,
Passed love and wisdom down to me
By the knowledge and guidance of my family tree.
I know I'm loved and looked over from above.

And I hope the branch I leave behind
Will be loving and strong for others to find,
Leaving love and guidance
That will weather any storm.

At One with All

So much love within my heart.
Beauty with love every day.
Beating out a sweet melody,
For the love that's been sent my way.
This love in my heart, forever growing,
Peace and calm each day I'm knowing.
All good things do me surround,
Love's fulfilment all abound.
Daily blessings – I have many;
Disbelief, doubts – I don't have any.
Not now I've seen the light myself,
Worth more to me than a ransom's wealth.

Peaceful Harmony

Angels of peace, come my way,
Help me live in love and harmony.
Goodwill to each and every man,
May he know much joy, throughout his span.
Every step may he walk in love,
And feel the heavenly rays from above.

May his heart be rich and full,
Overflowing with love for one and all.
Let his days be rich and fine,
Like an old fermented wine.
I pray every man be touched with peace,
May love and faith never cease.

Healing from Within

Let the healing start today,
Turn that cheek, be on your way.
Thus your heavy heart can be
Floating gently, light and free.

To forgive is hard, we know,
But until you do you cannot go
To the future that lies before;
Only you can open the door.

So leave behind all the sorrow,
Look forward to a new tomorrow.
All the sadness of the years
Holds you back and brings the tears.

Leave it all, make your new start,
Let love come from within your heart.
So forgive and begin to mend,
Bring your suffering to an end.

Make a start that's fresh and new,
Do it now – do it for you.
God will help you through the day,
Forgive – and go upon your way.

Hurting Inside

Tears that flow like rain on your cheeks
Come from deep down within.
And there in your heart,
The pain is such a burden to bear.
The ache in your heart only you can put right,
Find sweet peace and harmony, no more to fight.

Kind gentle life that flows like a stream,
Eyes that see beauty, this is my dream.
No more tears to fall down your face,
Rushing no more, life's not a race.
Ears that hear kind words
That make you smile.
Then comes peace
And all is worthwhile.

Seven Days

He took six days to create the world
And on the seventh, the Sabbath, did rest.
God gave and made such beauty,
He showed his love in rich abundance,
For he gave us his very best.

He gave man an important task
As the caretaker of this precious gift.
Man has somehow lost his way,
Now this planet's unbalanced and sick.
He trusted us with the birds and the trees.

Man looks the other way; he's no longer trying
For the things asked of him from the start;
God's precious creation, with love in his heart.
One day soon, if we're not more aware,
We'll take a look and it won't be there.

So open your eyes and look all around
At the beauty and wonders that do us surround.
God gave so much and was truly pleased,
He trusted us to care and love
This precious planet from our Father above.

Only Gone Next Door

If only we could tell them
That they're not so far away.
They've only gone on over
And we'll see them all one day.

Life goes on in spirit,
They're still around us every day.
We can go on feeling them near;
Open your heart, push aside the fear.

When you look at the wonders
That surround us every day,
You feel and know there's so much more,
It's not the end, just going through another door.

So open up your heart and feel
The wonders there in store.
Have more faith and just believe,
They've only gone next door.

Sweet Forgiveness

I bet when God looks down from above
He can hardly believe his eyes:
The conflict and the cruelty
That goes on beneath his skies.

Why is man so unforgiving
With much hate within his heart?
Where's all the love gone
That is born with us at the start?

If we could push the hate away,
And look to tomorrow, a fresh new day;
Cast the sadness, hate and sorrow aside,
Say 'This is my brother', say it with pride;

Then, at the end of a tiring day,
Put our heads on our pillows
And our prayers then say;
Pray for the lost, that they will be found,

And that peace and much love
Our whole world will surround;
Then, as our Father looks down from above,
He can sit back and smile at a job well done,
Knowing man lives in peace, as it's meant to be.

Words on Paper

As I sit and write these words,
My heart is full of sorrow.
So much conflict in the world,
No happy bright tomorrow?

Why, when there's so much beauty,
Must the ugly hate live on?
And all the mean selfishness
Take the place of harmony and love?

We're surrounded by much beauty,
From the flowers to the trees,
The sweetness of the drops of rain,
And the bird's sweet melodies.

Deep in thought, my heart is lifted
In the hope I see one day:
Love and harmony all around,
And much peace here to stay.

Twinkling Cover

There's a blanket of stars in the sky tonight,
They're shining out brightly, all sparkling white.
Like diamonds they twinkle in their special way,
Until it's time once more for day.

Come back bright stars tomorrow night,
Light up the skies with your twinkle so bright;
Just like the sky is looking over me,
Shining over creation for all to see.

Tranquillity

Softly, doves of peace,
Go upon your way;
Showing love and peace,
Help us on our way.

Pure and white and wise,
Doing all they can.
What a prize example,
Trying to show man.

Gentle doves of peace,
Flying over all creation,
Spreading all their peace,
To each and every nation.

Uncaring

Oh dear me, what have we done?
Destroying the ozone, our shield from the sun.
Earth's great sunshade, nearly gone,
Will this be the end, or will we go on?

All the warnings we've had in the past,
Told over and over, it won't last.
The Earth is such a beautiful place,
We're the caretakers, what a disgrace.

We should have cared and tended it more,
No more now this safety door.
The Earth is truly a beautiful plain,
But there's damage being done by acid rain.

My heart is sad, it's full of tears;
Can we last, are there many more years?
The trees and flowers are losing their sheen,
There's a dullness about, no longer lush green.

Our planet cries out, in so much pain,
Stop this destruction, this acid rain.
We were entrusted to love and to care.
Why don't they hear, is there anyone there?

Same Difference

Everyone is different,
But we're basically the same.
We all like to laugh,
But cry out when we're in pain.

We live by rules
That others make.
Sometimes they don't work,
There are often mistakes.

Each one of us
Is an individual.
But they treat us
Like we're one.

Some can't eat everyday food,
It makes them very ill.
Although we might look alike,
We're different there within.

What suits one of us
Can put another in a spin.
Because we are so different,
That's what makes us what we are.

I am an individual,
A person, this I am.
I'll always do things my way,
All my days till the end of my span.

Taking a Break

All the flowers are going to sleep,
As the night creeps over the day.
Their heads are gently drooping,
As the breeze it makes them sway.

All the pretty colours,
In magnificent hooray.
What a lovely sight it's been,
To brighten up our day.

Take a well-earned rest, flowers,
Come back again tomorrow.
Lift up all our hearts so high,
Especially those with sorrow.

Sent with Love

Just a man who was sent with love,
Ever there to lend a hand,
Show compassion and understand,
Give universal love for all;
Surround us with a love so full.

Understanding Creation

Gentle, blessèd, guiding hand,
Oceans of blue, green of the land,
Does anyone really understand?

Mr Moon and Friends

I see the moon smiling at me,
Soft misty smile, so high and so free.
Up above the world to survey,
Seeing night gently turn to day.

Bright moon so mysterious,
With stars among your friends.
Out there in endless space,
Going on and on with no end.

All the different planets,
Up there so very high,
Helping to make up the universe,
And decorate the sky.

The man in the moon
Has a beaming smile on his face,
As he looks down on the world,
And sees such a wonderful place.

All God's creation, truly such a wonder,
Brightness of the sunshine,
Such power of the thunder.
Shine on, Mr Moon, with your friends above,
What a great creation, given with such love.

We Are

We are what we are,
In the world of man.
All part and parcel
Of the great mighty plan.

Each one is different,
With characteristics all his own.
Some stay in one place,
And others choose to roam.

Man has a spirit,
Along with his free will.
He can be good or bad,
Many things all in one.

Such a complete creation,
Created with much love.
Each one so very different,
Sent and given from above.

Grow and Prosper

We could help this world of ours,
Just by giving and sharing,
Spreading a little kindness,
And smiling to show we care.

Break a fresh-baked loaf in half,
And share your daily bread.
Help someone along the path,
Turn him away from fear and dread.

Feel that inner warmth inside
As you give a helping hand.
Feel the deep sense of pride,
Let's try to understand.

What a happy smiling world
Could be with us day by day.
If only we could give and take,
And find the right words to say.

If Only

Oh, if I could see you,
And tell you one more time
Just how much I love you
And of the pain you've left behind.

Oh, so many happy days –
Now they're gone, left me in a haze.
Feeling lost, still needing you,
Want you here to help me through.

Heart so broken, will it mend?
Know for sure it's not the end.
We will all meet up again
With many tears of joy; gone will be this pain.

Friendship

There, in you, I have a friend,
One who cares, on whom I can depend,
Always there with an outreaching hand,
With gentle words that understand.

So many mysteries we don't know,
We go forward, it's far to go.
Much to cope with every day,
Not always having things our way.

Many lessons for us to learn,
Every point we have to earn.
Makes our journey easier to bear,
Knowing friends like you are there.

As some days seem rather long,
Your support will make me strong.
Someone who'll stand by my side,
To call a friend with love and pride.

Cluster of Light

There's a cluster of stars
Shining down on me,
Like beautiful diamonds
For all to see.

Twinkling and shining,
Helping light up the dark.
Soft shadows falling
On the still of the night.

Gentle silhouettes,
Creeping from the still,
The quiet of the night
Silently to fill.

Catch a star
And put it safely away.
Then you can survey it
In the gentle light of day.

Not quite as shiny
As it was up in the sky,
But still a thing of beauty,
So pleasing to the eye.

Shine on, you cluster,
In the sky up above.
Thanks for the pleasure you give,
As you shine out with love.

Get Wise

Men with riches and with power,
High up there within your towers,
You may have wealth, but you're not wise
As you live your grandiose lives.

You can't buy wisdom, it don't come in packs,
This, I'm afraid, is what your life lacks.
Our planet is dying, it cries out in pain,
From stifling pollution and cruel acid rain.

The earth is a gift, like a rare precious jewel,
To be cared for and loved, not treated so cruel.
Breathtaking and precious, this is our Earth,
No price could ever be put on its worth.

So much beauty, all given with love,
From our Father, Almighty God.
But this gift is being badly abused.
Man is misguided, it's all being misused.

Every day, if you open wide your eyes,
Things will astound, leaving a sweet surprise.
Notice the trees, how they gently sway,
Taking and cleaning the air every day.

Our planet falls deeper into destitution,
Due to profit and all this pollution.
Let's act now, time marches on,
Leave it much longer and all will be gone.

Hear Earth's cries as it rumbles and quakes,
It tries to tell us and gives us a shake.
We see the signs, but we don't heed,
The time has come to act with speed.

So open wide your eyes and heart,
Let's act now and make a start.
No more Earth will quake with sorrow,
Earth and man could share a bright tomorrow.

Sharing a Smile

Stop for a moment,
Just for a while,
Will you return
Somebody's smile?

Will you cheer
Somebody's day,
As they go
Upon their way?

Now going forward,
With heart so light,
Future is clearer
And so bright.

Sharing a smile
Is a lovely thing.
And, best of all,
It doesn't cost a thing.

Dig for It

Oh yes, there is much love in the world,
We just have to dig to find it.
There is plenty to go around,
It's in our actions and our sounds.

Sometimes we feel a little shy,
With words often unspoken.
We fear and hold back,
Afraid to show our love.

If you can't speak, then give a little token.
A flower is a beautiful thing
And, when given with love, is special.
So try to spread a little love.

There's plenty to go around.
Give it in your actions,
Or in words with a sweet sound;
It's there, it's all around.

Dig deep in your heart and you will know,
You'll feel it rise and overflow
So you can share it every day,
Then you'll know you've found the way.

His Gift to Us

Our Lord, to us, gave his son,
To walk with us upon the Earth.
He was his only precious son,
This was the purpose of his birth.

He shared his wisdom and his love,
This gift to us from up above.
He saw the sin and felt the pain,
This was a very sad refrain.

His Father gave the world in peace,
With endless beauty, never to cease.
Man strayed far from God's chosen path –
He took it all, not content with half.

The greed it overtook it all,
Man's eyes were closed – the arrogant fool!
They put him to the cross that day,
And then he took our sins away.

We didn't learn, it still goes on,
The wars and conflicts, cruel and long.
We had it all, needing only love,
The gifts sent from our Father, God.

We've bruised the Earth and it feels down,
The acid rain makes it frown.
No more the sun to kiss your face,
Out there can be an unsafe place.

I bet our Father sheds a tear
For all the things that he holds dear.
Let's show respect and tend with love
This gift sent from the Lord above.

Man still goes on, his profits to make,
He rarely gives, but often takes.
Wake up and hear Earth's humble plea,
'Be kind and show some love to me.'

Our Precious Gifts

Many things before us lie,
Sometimes we laugh,
Other times we cry.
Many things lie on life's path.

Life can be kind,
Other times quite cruel.
It doesn't have
Any hard and fast rules.

Our children are a precious gift
That we tend with loving care.
They are a continuation of us,
And with them we closely share

All their smiles and their tears,
As so swiftly pass the years.
And with pride we see them grow,
Love in our heart, warmth from its glow.

We feel their worries and their pain,
Standing strong by their side.
As we watch with love and pride,
Often our tears we have to hide.

When they are down and need us most,
We give to them our very best.
Passing on love, in words and deeds,
We try to meet their every need.

We pray for strength to pass it on,
And share what's in our hearts.
For these are our precious gifts,
Of us they are a part.

Inner Glow

Come to me on a winter's night,
Soft and gentle, sweet delight.
Know that I wait for you,
With a heart that's loyal and true.

Come to me when the snow is around,
White and crisp upon the ground.
Feel the chill within the air,
But I am warm because you're there.

Who's there?

All of a sudden, I am aware
I'm not alone, there's somebody there.
Peace and calm comes all over me.
I feel contented, so happy and free.

All of a sudden, I'm no longer alone.
Love, it surrounds me, so tender and true.
Blessèd the day that you came to my side.
From all of the wonder I no longer hide.

With you by my side we'll walk many paths,
Together for ever in love and in trust.
All of a sudden, I am aware
Of this wonderful feeling that I want to share.

Those Who

There are those who
Heard the words so wise.
Those who still looked
With tight-closed eyes.

Those who were loved
And touched by you.
Those who saw love
Come pouring through.

Those who heard second hand
Of the unselfishness so true.
Those who heard of the wisdom,
Rightfully bestowed on you.

Remembering our Garden

In a lovely garden,
Many years ago,
A man planted seeds,
And waited for them to grow.

Such pretty colours,
Reaching from each stem.
This man shared love,
Was gentle among men.

Such a pretty garden,
So long, long ago.
Growing such lovely flowers,
In a garden I did know.

All the radiant colours
That were tended with such love.
Each flower a creation,
From our Father, God above.

Dear Richard
              I hope you enjoy these
Poems and Share them with others.
To Hopefully uplift and enlighten.
          Love & Light
              from
                  Irene x

Printed in the United Kingdom
by Lightning Source UK Ltd.
120666UK00001B/319-339